CAROLINA
PANTHERS

SportsZone

An Imprint of Abdo Publishing
abdopublishing.com

BY TODD KORTEMEIER

abdopublishing.com

Published by Abdo Publishing, a division of ABDO, PO Box 398166, Minneapolis, Minnesota 55439. Copyright © 2017 by Abdo Consulting Group, Inc. International copyrights reserved in all countries. No part of this book may be reproduced in any form without written permission from the publisher. SportsZone™ is a trademark and logo of Abdo Publishing.

Printed in the United States of America, North Mankato, Minnesota
042016
092016

Cover Photo: Jeff Haynes/AP Images
Interior Photos: Jeff Haynes/AP Images, 1; James A. Finley/AP Images, 4-5; David Drapkin/ AP Images, 6; Kevin Reece/AP Images, 7; Amy Sancetta/AP Images, 8-9; John Zich/AP Images, 10-11; Al Golub/AP Images, 12-13, 14; Chuck Burton/AP Images, 15; Paul Sakuma/AP Images, 16-17; Mark Humphrey/AP Images, 18-19; Charles Rex Arbogast/AP Images, 20; Mike McCarn/ AP Images, 21; Rick Havner/AP Images, 22-23; Matt York/AP Images, 24-25; Rainier Ehrhardt/AP Images, 26; David Goldman/AP Images, 27; Julie Jacobson/AP Images, 28-29

Editor: Patrick Donnelly
Series Designer: Nikki Farinella

Cataloging-in-Publication Data
Names: Kortemeier, Todd, author.
Title: Carolina Panthers / by Todd Kortemeier.
Description: Minneapolis, MN : Abdo Publishing, [2017] | Series: NFL up close | Includes index.
Identifiers: LCCN 2015960358 | ISBN 9781680782103 (lib. bdg.) | ISBN 9781680776218 (ebook)
Subjects: LCSH: Carolina Panthers (Football team)--History--Juvenile literature. | National Football League--Juvenile literature. | Football--Juvenile literature. | Professional sports--Juvenile literature. | Football teams-- South Carolina--Juvenile literature.
Classification: DDC 796.332--dc23
LC record available at http://lccn.loc.gov/2015960358

TABLE OF CONTENTS

CARDIAC CATS

In 2003, the Carolina Panthers mastered the art of winning close games. Including the playoffs, 14 of their 20 games were decided by six points or fewer. Nervous Panthers fans began calling them "The Cardiac Cats" for the heart-stopping drama at the end of most of their games.

One of their most exciting games was in the playoffs against the St. Louis Rams. The Panthers led by 11 points with less than three minutes to go, but the Rams tied it on a last-second field goal. In overtime, each team had a chance to win but missed a field goal. Then the Panthers won it with a long touchdown pass on the first play of the second overtime period.

Members of the Panthers celebrate after their double-overtime playoff victory over the St. Louis Rams.

A week later, the Panthers upset the Philadelphia Eagles to reach the Super Bowl for the first time. The New England Patriots came into the game as seven-point favorites. And they came out strong. But the Panthers kept answering.

With a little over a minute to go, Carolina quarterback Jake Delhomme hit wide receiver Ricky Proehl for a 12-yard touchdown. The extra-point kick tied the game 29-29. It looked like the Cardiac Cats might force the Super Bowl into overtime for the first time ever.

Panthers quarterback Jake Delhomme throws a pass against the New England Patriots in the Super Bowl.

Ricky Proehl's game-tying touchdown late in the fourth quarter gave the Panthers' championship hopes a boost.

The Panthers defense was strong, but it could not stop Tom Brady. The Patriots quarterback led a last-minute drive to get in field goal range. Kicker Adam Vinatieri made a 41-yard field goal to win it for New England. Even though they fell short, the Panthers had given their fans a season to remember.

Jake Delhomme's expression sums up the frustrations of the Panthers and their fans after losing to the Patriots in the Super Bowl.

EARLY DAYS

The Carolina Panthers were officially announced as the 29th National Football League (NFL) team on October 26, 1993. They would begin play in 1995. The city of Charlotte celebrated with a fireworks show. Fans had already shown their support, buying more than 40,000 season tickets.

FAST FACT

Panthers owner Jerry Richardson played for the Baltimore Colts and caught a touchdown pass in the 1959 NFL Championship Game.

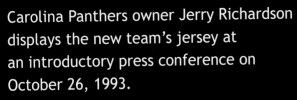

Carolina Panthers owner Jerry Richardson displays the new team's jersey at an introductory press conference on October 26, 1993.

Kerry Collins and the Panthers won the
NFC West Division in 1996, their second
year in the NFL.

Like most expansion teams, the Panthers started off slow. They opened the 1995 season by going 0-5. But they won 7 of their last 11 games that year. That set them up for a breakthrough second season. They went 12-4 and made it to within one game of the Super Bowl.

Superstar pass rusher Kevin Greene led a strong Panthers defense. They allowed only 218 points in 1996, the fewest in team history. Even though the Panthers lost to the Green Bay Packers in the National Football Conference (NFC) Championship Game, fans were excited. Few had expected the team to be this good this fast.

ROCK BOTTOM

Fans were eager for the Panthers to take the next step in 1997. Instead, the team struggled to build on its success in 1996. The Panthers went 7-9 in 1997 and 4-12 in 1998. It was time for a change. Carolina hired two-time Super Bowl champion coach George Seifert in 1999.

George Seifert, *left*, helped Steve Beuerlein put up some great numbers in the Panthers' offense.

Linebacker Sam Mills was a veteran leader for Carolina in the team's first three seasons.

FAST FACT

Sam Mills's 51 is the only retired number in team history. The linebacker played for the Panthers from 1995 through 1997.

Despite having some star players to work with, Seifert could not turn the Panthers around. Quarterback Steve Beuerlein led the NFL with 4,436 passing yards in 1999. Wide receiver Muhsin Muhammad topped 1,000 receiving yards in 1999 and 2000. But the Panthers won only 16 games in three seasons under Seifert. They bottomed out with a disastrous 1-15 season in 2001.

The Panthers turned to coach John Fox in 2002. He soon put together a core group of players to lead the Panthers back to success.

Panthers receiver Muhsin Muhammad breaks a tackle in a 2001 game against the San Francisco 49ers.

FOX GETS RESULTS

John Fox came to Carolina from the New York Giants. He was a successful defensive coordinator there. He improved the Panthers' defense right away. Under Fox, the Panthers regularly ranked in the top 10 for fewest points and yards allowed. Defensive end Julius Peppers was one of the NFL's most dangerous pass rushers.

FAST FACT

The Panthers played their first season at Memorial Stadium in Clemson, South Carolina. Their current home, Bank of America Stadium, opened in 1996 in Charlotte.

Coach John Fox congratulates Julius Peppers, *90*, after Peppers intercepted a Dallas Cowboys pass in the 2003 playoffs.

Receiver Steve Smith emerged as one of the best players in Panthers history. Drafted in 2001, he thrived under Fox and formed a dangerous duo with quarterback Jake Delhomme. Smith regularly was among league leaders in catches and yards.

In 2003, the Panthers had their best season yet. Smith and Delhomme hooked up for a 69-yard touchdown to win their double-overtime playoff game in St. Louis that year. Then the Panthers reached the Super Bowl for the first time.

Steve Smith rejoices after scoring the game-winning touchdown in double overtime against the St. Louis Rams.

Jake Delhomme, *left*, and Steve Smith played together in Carolina from 2003 to 2009.

FAST FACT

Steve Smith is the Panthers' all-time leader in receiving yards with 12,197.

The Panthers got back to the NFC Championship Game in 2005, but they lost to the Seattle Seahawks 34-14. In 2008, they matched their best record ever at 12-4. However, the Arizona Cardinals upset them in the first round of the playoffs.

After a 2-14 season in 2010, the Panthers decided it was time for a new coach. Ron Rivera had served as a defensive coordinator for two NFL teams. He was brought in as part of a defensive revival in Carolina. The Panthers also used their top draft pick the next year to bring a game-changing quarterback to town.

Ron Rivera was the Panthers' rookie head coach in 2011.

Cam Newton, *left*, was roughed up by the
Cardinals in his first NFL start. But better times
were ahead for him and the Panthers.

SUPERCAM

The Panthers selected quarterback Cam Newton with the first pick in the 2011 NFL Draft. Newton had won the Heisman Trophy that season while leading the Auburn Tigers to the college football national championship.

Newton struggled adjusting to the NFL at first. But with help from the league's second-ranked defense, he led the Panthers to the playoffs in his third season. Linebacker Luke Kuechly was named the NFL Defensive Player of the Year that season. That was a sign of good things to come.

Carolina got on a roll in 2015, and Newton deserved much of the credit. The Panthers won their first 14 games and finished the regular season 15-1. Newton threw a career-high 35 touchdown passes and was intercepted just 10 times. He also made a big impact on the ground, rushing for 636 yards and 10 touchdowns. For his efforts, he won the NFL Most Valuable Player (MVP) Award.

Luke Kuechly, *59*, was the NFL Defensive Rookie of the Year in 2012.

Cam Newton hands a ball to a happy fan after scoring a touchdown in 2015.

Cam Newton threw and ran himself into the record books against the New York Giants on December 20, 2015.

The Panthers rolled through the NFC playoffs to reach their second Super Bowl. The Denver Broncos' defense was too tough, however. Their pass rushers gave Newton a hard time. Carolina never got its offense going. The defense played well, but Newton fumbled twice, and the Broncos scored touchdowns off both turnovers.

Carolina's amazing season ended with a 24-10 loss in the Super Bowl. But with Newton leading the offense, Kuechly driving the defense, and Rivera in control on the sidelines, the future never looked brighter in Carolina.

FAST FACT

On December 20, 2015, Cam Newton became the first quarterback in NFL history to have at least 340 passing yards and 100 rushing yards in the same game.

TIMELINE

1993

The Carolina Panthers are officially announced as the NFL's 29th team.

1995

The Panthers finish strong and post a 7-9 record in their first season.

1996

Bank of America Stadium opens in Charlotte.

1996

After winning 12 regular-season games, the Panthers reach the NFC Championship Game before falling to the Green Bay Packers.

2004

The Panthers play in their first Super Bowl but lose to the New England Patriots 32-29 on February 1.

2006

The Panthers win two road playoff games in January before losing at Seattle in the NFC Championship Game.

2011

Carolina selects quarterback Cam Newton with the first overall pick in the NFL Draft.

2015

Newton wins the NFL MVP Award and the Panthers win 15 games, but they come up just short in the Super Bowl against the Denver Broncos.

GLOSSARY

CONFERENCE
A group of divisions that help form a league.

COORDINATOR
An assistant coach who is in charge of a team's offense or defense.

DRAFT
The process by which teams select players who are new to the league.

EXPANSION
When a league grows by adding new teams.

PLAYOFFS
A set of games played after the regular season that decides which team will be the champion.

SACK
A tackle of the quarterback behind the line of scrimmage before he can pass the ball.

WIDE RECEIVER
An offensive player whose main duty is to catch passes.

ABOUT THE AUTHOR

Todd Kortemeier has authored dozens of books for young people, primarily on sports topics. He is a graduate of the University of Minnesota's School of Journalism & Mass Communication and lives near Minneapolis with his wife.